Walkie Talkie Faith

JENNI SEDON

Copyright © 2025 All rights reserved.

No part of this book may be reproduced or transmitted in any form or by any means, electronic or mechanical, including photocopying, recording or by an information storage and retrieval system (except by a reviewer who may quote brief passages in a magazine, newspaper, or on the web) without permission in writing from the author.

Contents

Acknowledgements	1
Dedications	3
Introduction	5
PART 1	7
WALKIE TALKIE FAITH	
IN EVERYDAY LIFE	
1. WALKIE TALKIE FAITH	8
2. TESTING TESTING 1, 2, 3	11
3. HEART-LINE TO HEAVEN	17
4. ANYTIME, ANYWHERE	21
5. WHERE ARE MY RUNNERS?	25
6. AN UNANSWERED PRAYER	35
7. DETOURS	41
8. JOURNAL THE JOURNEY	51

9. TRUST AND OBEY	57
10. THAT SOUNDS FISHY	63
11. MY MOSES SPEECH	69
12. GIVE ME A SIGN	75
13. FRIDAY NIGHT AT THE SERVO	81
PART 2 WALKIE TALKIE FAITH DURING TRAGEDY	87
14. THE BLUE TARPAULIN	88
15. A NEEDLE IN A HAYSTACK	93
16. A SLIVER OF LIGHT	97
17. AN UNUSUAL CHRISTMAS CARD	99
18. FEATHERED FRIENDS	103
19. MESSAGE IN MOVIELAND	111
20. MY KNIGHT IN TARNISHED ARMOUR	113
21. THE ANCHOR HOLDS	119
22. FLAT BATTERY	123
23. MOURN NO MORE	129
24. OVER AND OUT	135

Acknowledgements

My sincere thanks to my dear friend, Madonna, for her love, support, and friendship over the years. This book would not have come to fruition without her tireless dedication and ability to decipher my meanderings and transform them into the written word.

And a huge "Thank you" to all my friends who have encouraged me on this long writing journey, especially Jan Ingram, Louise Ingram and Georgia Burr.

Most importantly, and at the risk of sounding like an Academy Award recipient, I acknowledge that without God, this book would not be possible. I don't know where I would be without His constant guidance, unconditional love, and walkie talkie conversations.

GHOSTWRITER/EDITOR: Madonna
ILLUSTRATOR: Eryanto

Dedications

Firstly, this book is dedicated to you, **the reader**.
May God bless you richly.

It is also dedicated to my beautiful grandchildren;
Reef, Isla, Jake and Freddie.

Introduction

Have you ever thought, *I can't see or hear God, so how do I know He's real? He's always been silent when I've most needed Him.* Honestly, I've often felt the same way.

In **Walkie Talkie Faith**, I share personal reflections about my friendship with God and how I learned to hear His voice by tuning to His frequency. That's where the Walkie Talkie analogy comes in. Are there still times I find it difficult to hear Him? Absolutely. I share these as well.

Walkie Talkie Faith is a bit of a mixed bag, like me. It is a blend of Memoir, Inspiration and Reflection. You will read about my experiences with God in everyday life and during tragedy. Some of my stories end with *Jen's Takeaway* (my reflections), and ***A Snack for the Road***, (inspiration for you).

As you meander through my stories, you will stumble upon my catchphrase, "God, you've got to be kidding me!" You will also notice I excel in two roles - *Expert Excuse-Maker* and *Inquisitive Inquirer*.

Does God respond to my excuses and questions with angry outbursts? Does He wring His hands and lament, **"Why, oh why, must you question me?"**

Walkie Talkie Faith is not a theological book. I believe God has made it easy for us to relate to Him and I hope my personal stories reflect the friendship God offers us all. I know I can ask God anything, much like you may ask a close friend, "Hey, does this outfit look okay? Honest answer, please."

PART 1

WALKIE TALKIE FAITH

IN EVERYDAY LIFE

CHAPTER ONE

WALKIE TALKIE FAITH

Why the name *Walkie Talkie Faith*? Because I've discovered that having a relationship with God is as simple and exciting as using a walkie talkie. As a child, I recall playing with walkie talkies. My two sisters, my brother and I dashed about the yard, hollering and laughing, sending and receiving impromptu messages. I was amazed that at the click of a button, or the lift of a finger, we could chat with each other so easily and in such a novel way.

From an early age, I learned I could have a walkie talkie relationship with God. I could talk to Him about anything; mundane, serious, or in between. As a child, I never doubted God was speaking to me. Yet, as an adult, I sometimes allowed reason to override my childlike faith. Why would the God who created the universe want to speak to me?

Thankfully, over time, I became more adept at having two-way conversations with God. My walkie talkie is now heart-held rather than hand-held. I pour out my heart to God, the good, the bad and the ugly. In return, He offers unconditional love, wisdom and guidance. He is on the other end 24/7, rain, hail, or shine. When I talk, He always listens. When He talks to me, I sometimes listen. I wish I listened more because, when I do, life is so much easier.

As you read these stories, you will notice God spoke to me through many sources: His Word the Bible, nature, music, podcasts, movies, TV shows, a billboard, other people, books, intuition, hunches, ideas, dreams and visions.

You may read some of the stories in this book and think, *Hmm, that's just a coincidence, not God speaking.* We all have an individual relationship with God and relate to Him differently. I have learned the difference between a coincidence, and a God-incidence, because God and I have a unique relationship.

Do I always get it right? Definitely not. My walkie talkie journey has been, and still is, one of constant learning and discovery. Does this prevent me from believing God wants to speak to me? Not at all. It simply means I dig a little deeper for clarification when needed. I've discovered that humility and a willingness to learn are hallmarks of a vibrant walkie talkie life.

Is life a breeze because of my walkie talkie faith? Absolutely not. You will witness that in the following pages. I have had calamities in my life that most people will never experience. In fact, people have asked, "Why would you want anything to do with God after what happened?" My answer, "He is the one who walked beside me through the valley of the shadow of death."

I felt like a tiny boat amidst a tsunami when I lost our family home and my husband, Rick, on Christmas Day in 2006. My boat was tossed by waves of confusion, heartbreak, doubt and fear. My walkie talkie signal was so weak I could not muster a prayer. Thankfully, God's frequency receives spoken and unspoken prayer. He heard my desperate *SOS* call and rescued me from the raging sea, anchoring me in His love.

Perhaps you are wondering if this type of walkie talkie faith is exclusive to a select few. The answer is a resounding "No!" Anybody can have walkie talkie faith and walkie talkie time with God. In fact, He wants you to have this.

If you stop and take the time to connect to God's frequency you will hear His unique messages for you. Today may be the day you decide to pick up your walkie talkie and give it a go: "God, are you there? Over..."

> **For God speaks again and again, though people do not recognise it.** *Job 33:14 - TLB*

CHAPTER TWO

TESTING TESTING 1, 2, 3

My walkie talkie life with God began over 50 years ago. I was seven at the time, just a wee lass living in New Zealand. I clearly recall that amazing moment, my first heart-to-heart communication with God. Way back then I already believed in God, but I wanted to know Him better. I wanted Him to prove He was real. Being a child, with child-like faith, I concocted a plan for God to show me He was real.

One night, before going to bed, I placed three of my favourite lollies on my bedside table. I prayed a heartfelt prayer. "God, I have left out three lollies; one for you, one for Jesus and one for the Holy Spirit. I want you prove to me that you are real, so just take the lollies while I'm sleeping, please, and then I will know for sure that you are real."

I woke the following morning with great anticipation, followed by great disappointment. The three stooges were sitting there large as life. The only difference was my bedside table now displayed multi-coloured streaks. My seven-year-old mind worked overtime. It was obvious; God had tried the lollies and didn't like them. I wondered what his favourite lollies were and wished I had put them out instead. With all the skill of a budding Miss Marple I investigated those lollies inside, outside and upside down. I compared the colour, size, shape and texture of each, noting any small discrepancy. I imagined God popping the first lolly in His mouth, swirling it around and putting it back on the bedside table. The second and third lollies would have received the same treatment.

As I held the three discarded lollies in my hand I heard God's voice in my heart for the first time. It was not an external voice, nor was it a voice in my head. It seemed to come from the wall of my chest. It was strong and clear, **"Just because I didn't take the lollies doesn't mean I'm not real."** With my child-like faith I responded, "But, God, I just wanted you to prove to me that you are real." Again, the voice in my chest resonated, **"Just because I didn't take them doesn't mean I'm not real."**

My seven-year-old mind was not yet wise enough to conjure such words or possess such insight. I knew, without a doubt, God had spoken to me. I experienced an overwhelming sense of peace and the knowledge that God was real and wanted to communicate with me.

God did not answer my prayer the way I wanted Him to, but having a to-and-fro conversation with Him resulted in something more valuable - the beginning of my walkie talkie faith. My lolly experience taught me a vital lesson. My heart was the key to having a relationship with God. It was the transmitter that sent and received messages.

> **I call on you, my God, for you will answer me; turn your ear to me and hear my prayer.**
> PSALM 17:6 - NIV

My simple interaction with God, at such an early age, showed me that nobody is ever too young, or too old, to hear from God. Whether you are eight or ninety-eight God wants to speak to you. Because of my child-like faith I believed God was communicating with me; it was as simple as that.

Those of you who have children know how many questions they ask. We are God's children and He welcomes our wonderings.

If you are not used to communicating with God, or expecting Him to speak to you, here's a practical tip. You could start by reading, or listening to, a daily devotional.

It's easy to be distracted by the demands of life, so a daily devotional is a great place to start. You may be surprised how quickly you are inspired and revived simply by adding this to your day.

You can also talk to God, like you would talk to a new friend.

The Bible promises in Jeremiah 29:13 – **You will seek me and find me when you seek me with all your heart.**

Chapter Three

HEART-LINE TO HEAVEN

Did you know the Bible mentions the word *Heart* more than 900 times? Clearly, our hearts are important to God. He is a relational God and He wants us to have a heart-to-heart relationship with Him; one that is real, honest and genuine. If you are reading this, you fit the eligibility criteria. God wants to speak to you. He has probably spoken to you many times, but you may not have been tuned to His frequency.

You may recall trying to tune your radio to a particular station, and not quite hitting the mark. The result? Static and interference, a distinct cacophony that sets your teeth on edge. Because it's your favourite station you don't give up, you know it's just a matter of adjusting your dial the tiniest smidgeon. You persist and hit the mark, spot on. What a different experience. God is waiting for you to tune your frequency to His station.

Sometimes fear prevents us from tuning to God's frequency and listening for His voice. If you feel this way you may want to ask yourself where this fear originated. Perhaps you recall oddball religious characters portrayed in movies or on television. Maybe your church leaders discouraged you from listening for God's voice. You may have had harmful or negatives experiences with someone who called themselves a Christian.

Do people misrepresent God? Absolutely. Does this mean we should not have a heart-to-heart relationship with God and allow Him to speak to us? Absolutely not. God is not at fault because people have misrepresented Him. We are missing unparalleled adventure and joy if we allow fear and false-representation to keep us from a relationship with God. In fact, He is the only one who can fully understand you and heal the hurts people have caused.

Still think hearing from God all sounds a bit odd? You can be reassured you are hearing from God by using a simple test. God will never speak anything contrary to His Word, the Bible. If someone says God is telling them to do something that violates another person's free-will, or something that is clearly against God's laws or ways, that is not God speaking.

God speaks to us all differently because we all have a unique relationship with Him. Throughout this book you will see God often chose visions (pictures in my mind) or the gift of prophecy (knowing about something that will happen in the future) to speak to me. Visions and prophecy are gifts God gives to provide direction and encouragement to others. They are gifts given to serve others, not to glorify the person with the gifts.

1 Corinthians 12:7-11 and Acts 2:17

> **My heart has heard you say, "Come and talk with me." And my heart responds, "Lord, I am coming."** Psalm 27:8 - TLB

You may feel like a novice walkie talkie operator and not trust yourself, or others, to hear from God. If so, God has a reassuring promise for you.

> **You will seek me and find me when you seek me with all your heart.** JEREMIAH 29:31 NIV

Chapter Four

ANYTIME, ANYWHERE

Both my grandmothers loved jewellery which proved to be hereditary. By the age of eight I was saving to buy myself a diamond ring. This was not an easy task for an eight-year-old, but I was determined. After saving fastidiously, my piggy bank was overflowing and it was time to reap my reward. I purchased a stunning ring with one large crystal in the middle and two smaller crystals on either side. I admired it on my tiny hand day-in and day-out. I felt like a real princess.

When my grandmother came to visit I couldn't wait to show her my treasure. I flung out my tiny hand, "Nanna, it looks so real, doesn't it?" "It's lovely, dear, but it's not real. A genuine ring like that would be well out of your price range. You would never be able to afford it."

Regardless, the ring remained my prized possession, and although it might sound a little odd that simple ring became my best friend. As a child, I suffered from chronic asthma resulting in many days of missed school and many nights wheezing and struggling to breathe. I discovered that if I turned on my bedroom light the ring would catch the light, throwing a cascade of brilliant colours across the bedroom wall. My *light-shows-for-one* filled me with immense comfort and eased my fear and loneliness.

During one of those long, lonely nights I found myself sitting on the throne (toilet) admiring my treasure for the hundredth time. Even though I loved it dearly my grandmother's comments had stung. "God, I wish this ring was real," I cried. I knew He understood. He was my friend and I could talk to Him about anything.

The years rolled by, and my toy ring became less important. It was eventually misplaced and forgotten.

Many years later I was living in New Zealand and my boyfriend, Rick, and I were soon to be engaged. When the time came to choose an engagement ring I discovered my grandmother was right, real diamonds were expensive. We were on a limited budget as we were saving for a house. I settled for a ring that looked fabulous under the jeweller's bright lights but somehow lost its sparkle in the normal light of day. I tried to hide the fact I was disappointed with my engagement ring, but I suspect Rick may have known.

In 1993 Rick and I started our own business, a new and used furniture shop. From time to time he would attend estate jewellery auctions and surprise me with a diamond ring. Although the rings were beautiful none compared to my childhood ring and the feelings it evoked.

At one stage, we decided to travel to Brisbane to purchase stock for the shop. During this venture Rick spotted a magnificent diamond ring in a window display. Captivated by its beauty we excitedly entered the jewellery store. Its beauty came with a unique price tag; we could have purchased a house for the same amount.

Seeing the disappointment on our faces the jeweller told us he had a second-hand diamond out the back in his workshop. He escorted us to his apprentice jeweller's workroom which reminded me of Santa's workshop. It was filled with all manner of jewels, gems and glistening artefacts. Among these delights was the second-hand diamond. It was over one carat in weight.

Rick was immediately sold, while I contemplated the more practical aspects. Was the diamond real? Were they trying to rip us off? Should we be spending this much on a ring? Feeling faint, I looked around for somewhere to rest. I noticed a chair on the other side of the room and stumbled towards it. In stark contrast, Rick, full of exuberance, chatted with the jeweller about design options. I knew Rick had a natural flair for design, and a good eye for detail, so that was the least of my concerns. Amidst waves of nausea and dizziness I caught snippets of conversation. It was clear Rick was going ahead with the purchase. The ring would take some time to design so we paid up-front. The jeweller told us he would courier it to us when it was ready.

We returned to Townsville several thousand dollars poorer with nothing to show for it. Despite discouraging comments from friends Rick remained confident the jeweller would deliver on his promise. I felt like an expectant mother waiting for her baby to arrive. To my relief, after three long weeks, a courier phoned to say he would deliver the ring.

Was it worth the wait and angst? Absolutely. Rick and the jeweller had designed the perfect ring; one large diamond in the middle and two smaller diamonds on either side. I felt like a princess when I wore it. It was everything I had dreamed of and more. Rick and I had the ring valued and discovered it was worth five times the amount we paid.

Not long after receiving the ring I became sick with a tummy bug. I was sitting on the throne, annoyed I was so ill, when the light caught the facets of the diamond, causing them to dance in a kaleidoscope of colour across the wall. My mind clicked over reels from the past; this reminded me of something from my childhood. I recalled my tortuous nights struggling to breathe and my *light-shows-for-one*.

I heard the walkie talkie click and God's still small voice in my heart, **"Remember the ring you had as a child? Remember how you wanted a real diamond ring?"** Awestruck I realised two people, who knew nothing about my childhood ring, had created a genuine replica. God had honoured the long-forgotten prayer of a young girl, prayed in desperation some 30 years earlier!

I then received a second message. It consisted of just two words: ***"Anytime, anywhere."*** I chuckled to myself, seeing God's sense of humour. He was letting me know He could speak to me wherever and whenever He chose. I'd prayed my earnest childhood prayer on the throne, and He reminded me He'd answered it when I was on the throne.

Chapter Five

WHERE ARE MY RUNNERS?

Rick and I had been married two years. We were living in New Zealand and desperately wanted our own home. After saving fastidiously we had enough for a home deposit. Our dream home was situated in Gordonton outside Hamilton. We loved the tranquility of our quaint farmlet. Lush, green fields stretched for miles, dotted with dairy cows grazing lazily. Rick had a job as a fitter and turner at a local dairy company and I had a clerical job in Hamilton. We were part of a close-knit farming community and pot-luck dinners and get-togethers were frequent.

While attending a community pot-luck dinner I overheard some women talking about an inter-denominational Christian prayer group for ladies. Their joy and enthusiasm intrigued me. I envied their excitement and hoped I would be able to join them one day but my working hours prevented it at that time.

Five years later, after having our first child, my initial adventure was to the ladies prayer group with my beautiful baby girl. I was not used to the logistics of an outing with a baby; loading the baby capsule, packing a nappy bag, a pram and of course my precious girl. I was soon to discover I should have packed running shoes.

Lyn, the group leader, began by asking us to be still and quiet. She said we could ask God to give us an encouraging message for one of the other ladies. This was a new concept to me and it seemed strange and scary. I was more familiar with a traditional type of faith, not one where I sat and waited for God to speak to me. My prayer times consisted of bringing my shopping list to God. I punched in my order and waited for my *Divine Door-Dash Deliverer* to arrive.

I realised my footwear would certainly not withstand the type of sprint I suddenly had in mind. With no running shoes, and a baby in tow, I wasn't going anywhere.

I was grateful for all the toddlers and young children running in and out, up and down, screaming and laughing on top note. The ladies in the group also enjoyed a good natter and I could not imagine them drawing breath long enough to be still and quiet. I chuckled to myself. It was impossible for us to hear our own thoughts, let alone God's thoughts.

Surprisingly, one lady did tune in on her walkie talkie long enough to receive a message. While I can't recall the message, due to the passage of time, I certainly recall being bathed in a sense of peace as she spoke.

I recall being jolted back to reality as Lyn spoke about yet another foreign concept - spiritual gifts. She said we all had a spiritual gift or gifts given to us by God to encourage ourselves and other people. Because I was the newbie she asked the ladies to pray for me before the next meeting and ask God about my spiritual gifts. I imagined being gifted with a Volvo or a Porsche, but I was probably on the wrong track.

I left that day uncertain if I would return. Frankly, it all sounded quite odd. My adult relationship with God had always consisted of me doing all the talking and God doing all the listening.

When I arrived home I fell on my knees and pressed the *Help* button on my walkie talkie. I cried out, "God, these ladies all seem so lovely but I'm not sure about waiting in prayer for you to speak. I'm happy to give it a go if you would do one thing for me. I need you to confirm anything you say to me not once, but twice. I'm sorry to do this to you, but I don't want to be led astray." I wanted any messages the ladies received for me to be from God. My prayer was direct and came from a sincere heart.

A few days later I bumped into an older Christian lady from a very traditional Baptist Church. As we chatted I mentioned this new concept of listening to God in prayer. Surely she would think it was strange. She didn't seem at all shocked so I continued to tell her about my deal with God. Her response left me flabbergasted. "That's okay, dear. In the Bible Gideon asked God for confirmation too. " I didn't know much about Gideon, but I instantly liked Him. I had anticipated her berating me with 101 reasons why I shouldn't be involved with such a group, but instead she responded kindly and thoughtfully. For this, I will be eternally grateful.

I spent the following week questioning God about my spiritual gifts of a Volvo or a Porsche but He did not seem to be listening. On the morning of the prayer group my walkie talkie clicked. **"You are not going to know what your spiritual gifts are today."** At first, I thought my imagination was running wild. Was this a Jen thought or a God thought? It was certainly a strange message. Why would God talk to me to tell me He wasn't going to talk to me? The odd message came to me again, loud and clear. However, I was in such a rush to get my baby girl and myself out the door I didn't fully comprehend God had actually spoken to me.

In hindsight, He had spoken to me just as He had when I was a young girl. His voice was not a voice in my head, or my imagination, but a voice that felt like it was coming from my chest or heart area. Sadly, my first inclination was to reason away the possibility God could be speaking to me. I recalled the young girl and her *Lolly Test*. I was inspired by her simple faith. She had no doubt God would make Himself real to her.

I returned to prayer group the following week and the ladies said they had prayed about my spiritual gifts. When asked to share what they had received there was not a single comment about my spiritual gifts. The first lady said God had told her I was like Peter, one of Jesus' disciples. I thought, *Sorry lady, you've got it wrong. I would rather be like the Disciple Paul.* Then another lady read a verse she had received when praying, *Matthew 16:18* which is about Peter. Of course, by this stage, I was thinking they had met during the week. Then a third lady piped up and read what she had received during the week. It was from *Matthew 16* as well and was about Peter. The ladies were stunned and excited. It was obvious they had not conspired to make this happen. However, I couldn't help but wonder, *Is this a coincidence or a God-incidence?*

I wondered why there was such a focus on Peter. Obviously, God was letting me know loud and clear I had qualities like Peter even though I would have preferred to be like Paul. I had always admired Paul's faith. However, I did know that, like Peter, I could be irrational and impulsive. However, Peter was willing to have a go and step out, even at the risk of appearing foolish. Peter made mistakes. In fact, he denied Jesus three times prior to His death, but Jesus saw Peter's heart above all else. I finally understood the comparison and was grateful for the three words of confirmation.

Receiving these three simple messages marked the beginning of a new adventure with God and the beginning of the realisation that what I had thought were coincidences were actually God-incidences.

I learned some life-changing lessons from ladies group. Firstly, God had spoken into my heart just as He had when I was a child. I had not recognised His voice because the message didn't make sense to me, and because I had been too busy and distracted to reflect on its meaning. I wondered how many walkie talkie conversations I had missed over the years. How many times had I allowed logic to activate the **Mute** button on my walkie talkie?

Those wonderful ladies showed me God could use other people to speak to me, and vice versa. I also discovered I could deliberately set aside time for reciprocal conversations with God which was a totally new concept for me.

I was to learn the heavenly peace I felt that day was also God communicating with me. Many times since then I have experienced this peace, or lack thereof, when deciding on a course of action. I liken it to a gentle nudge or a cozy hug from God.

These simple yet profound lessons marked a turning point in my relationship with God. My walkie talkie times became a regular occurrence and my relationship with God began to deepen. I was beginning to recognise His voice more and more.

Sometimes God uses other people to guide us. Samuel was a young boy when he heard God's voice for the first time. However, he didn't realise God was speaking to him. A much older Christian, Eli, helped him to recognise God's voice and follow through on what God was asking him to do. Read **1 Samuel 3:7-11** if you'd like to know the whole story.

Throughout our lives, we transition between various roles. We can be teacher, student, or both.

Is God asking you to be a Samuel or an Eli?

CHAPTER SIX

AN UNANSWERED PRAYER

Have you ever felt disillusioned because God didn't answer your prayers? I sure have. Do I believe in the power of prayer? Absolutely. I have many stories of answered prayer. However, this is not one of them.

It all began when a close childhood friend announced her engagement to an ex-sailor. I wanted to feel excited, but instead I felt terribly uneasy. I had a feeling she was marrying the wrong man. He was a nice fellow when he wasn't drinking excessively, or hanging out at the pub with his mates. If this was how he acted pre-marriage I wondered what it would be like for my friend after they tied the knot. I was also worried she would be isolated as they would be living in a new town where she barely knew anyone.

My parents were also concerned for my friend, recalling the first time they met her husband-to-be at a mutual friend's wedding. He decided to perform the age-old party trick: *I shall sit in a corner and drink beer from my boot*. Surely, this was another sign to give her sailor a wide berth.

Desperate situations require desperate measures. So I pressed the **Desperation** button on my walkie talkie and begged God to intervene. I asked Him to stop the wedding. I waited expectantly for a phone call from my friend announcing she had seen the light and called off the wedding.

The wedding day arrived. I remember saying to God, "I know you have heard my prayers and there's nothing more I can do. I'm a tad confused here, Lord, but I'm just going to have to trust you know best." Imagine that - God knowing best!

I also experienced an incredible sense of peace, a peace that defied logic. It was the peace that only God can give, that gentle nudge reminding me everything would be okay.

Barely six months later their marriage was on the rocks. My friend remained in the marriage wondering why she had not heeded the warning signs. My prediction had been accurate; she was barely a blip on his radar once they were married. Going to the pub, drinking beer, and hanging out with his mates were high on his priority list, she wasn't.

When she was invited to church by a co-worker she gladly accepted, more out of sheer loneliness than a desire to go to church. She was not a Christian, or a churchgoer, but appreciated the kind offer of friendship.

That morning in church my friend experienced something completely new. She could not explain or understand what had happened; she felt the presence of God. Any of you who have experienced this will know how she felt. She came home from church with tear-stained cheeks, unable to explain to her husband why she had been so moved.

The next Sunday morning my friend wanted to attend church again. As she was about to step into the car she noticed her disapproving husband trailing behind her. "I'm coming to have words with those people who made you cry last week." She was a little concerned imagining him telling off the pastor and finishing off the communion wine in a boot.

That Sunday morning they entered the church, unaware their lives were about to change forever. My friend did not have the same experience she had the previous week - her husband did. He made the decision that day to ask Jesus to be Lord of his life. He didn't need to tell those church people off after all.

His life now had a different purpose and he was fulfilled as never before. This man, who had consumed alcohol religiously, went from drinking in pubs to telling people in pubs about Jesus. He and his wife both spent time in full-time ministry before starting a family. He has been a wonderful husband to my friend for over 40 years.

Imagine the outcome if God had answered my desperate walkie talkie prayer and ended their relationship. Never, in my wildest dreams, did I think a man who was so fond of the drink could have his life changed so dramatically simply by attending church once.

I later discovered his grandmother had been praying for Him fervently for many years. God had obviously answered *her* walkie talkie prayers.

> **This plan of mine is not what you would work out, neither are my thoughts the same as yours. For just as the heavens are higher than the earth, so are my ways higher than yours, and my thoughts than yours.** ISAIAH 55:8-9 - TLB

I realised my Walkie Talkie Faith was not about praying the right prayer. It was about my heart-to-heart relationship with God where I shared my thoughts and feelings, prayed in a specific direction, and then left the outcome to Him. It meant taking my finger off the **Control** button. We can become so blinkered we forget God sees the whole picture and knows the best possible outcome.

Importantly, I learned God spoke to me by giving me His peace. Even though my prayers weren't answered, God's peace was the gentle nudge reminding me everything would be okay. It surpassed logic and rational thought.

Are you in a situation that seems hopeless?

Have you considered taking your finger off the **Control** button and trusting God knows best?

He wants to give you His peace, the peace that passes understanding.

> **And the peace of God, which transcends all understanding, will guard your hearts and your minds in Christ Jesus.**
> PHILIPPIANS 4:7 – NIV

Chapter Seven

DETOURS

After seven long years of renovations our home in the Waikato, New Zealand, was finished to our satisfaction. I attended the ladies prayer group weekly. My knowledge of God, and my faith in Him, grew significantly because of those wonderful ladies. We were a close-knit group sharing our successes, failures and secrets.

One day God decided to place a detour across my path. It came in the form of a word of knowledge (an inspired message from God) from one of the ladies in the prayer group. The message was that I had reached cross-roads and would be heading in a different direction. I remember muttering to myself, "There is no way that's going to happen. I love my life here."

Soon after, Rick became restless and mentioned the possibility of moving across the Tasman to a Land Down Under. I was not prepared to move without gaining a higher perspective, so I grabbed my walkie talkie.

Over the coming weeks, my attitude towards our home notably changed. I started to notice the odd mark or two on our freshly painted walls. The road noise, which had not bothered me, now seemed annoying and incessant. The remoteness of the farmlet was becoming an inconvenience, whereas it had once been an appealing factor. I also started to have an inner peace about moving. I recalled the prayer group and the cross-roads message. It was beginning to look like we could be moving to Australia.

Before we left the prayer group the ladies held a farewell luncheon for me. Nothing had changed in the *Nattering Department* and I was worried there would not be time for them to pray with me - my, how things change! I recalled how recently I had wanted to *Run Run Run* at the thought of those wonderful ladies praying for me. I hoped there would be time for prayer as I desperately wanted and needed guidance for our future.

While we were still having lunch an image popped into my mind. The image was a map marked with a dot. I realised it was a map of Australia. I was unfamiliar with Australia and mentioned the vision to the ladies. I sketched a rough outline of what I had seen. One of the ladies said, "Oh, the dot is where Mount Isa is." I asked, "What's there?" I found her response less than reassuring. "Lots of red dust." I thought to myself, *There's no way we'll be going there. Asthma and dust aren't a great combination.* I did not mention the vision, the dot, or Mount Isa to Rick or anybody else. It didn't seem relevant and I put it out of my mind.

In a few short months we were selling our house and belongings and moving to Australia. It is no mean feat leaving home and country, family, and friends, with two small girls aged one and three. To complicate the situation further Rick did not have a job in Australia, and we had no idea where we would be living. You are most likely beginning to get the picture.

Our first stop in Australia was Sydney. We planned to stay for a week and have a mini-holiday after our move across the Tasman. We stayed on the outskirts in a cabin and after purchasing a car we moved on.

We then travelled north to Coffs Harbour as we had heard it was a gorgeous place to live. This was certainly true, with its many beautiful beaches along the coastline. We were concerned about the use of chemicals on the local banana plantations, and the possibility they could adversely impact the health of our young girls. So, in the words of Willy Nelson we were *On the Road Again,* this time heading further north to Mackay.

Mackay had intrigued me since childhood. When I was at primary school in New Zealand, a teacher from Mackay came for a short stay. She told us North Queensland was warm and sunny all year round. I couldn't believe such a place existed and a desire to live in the tropics was ignited.

No offence to Mackay dwellers, but it just wasn't the place for us. Rick and I knew this as soon as we arrived. It wasn't that we disliked Mackay, it just wasn't right for us.

We had very dear friends in New Zealand who, at one stage, had lived in the tropics in a place called Townsville. They had always spoken fondly about Townsville and its relaxed lifestyle. So we set off again, travelling even further north to Townsville. I imagined snorkelling on the Barrier Reef, pristine white beaches, sparkling oceans, and the girls building sandcastles. Maybe this move would be a gorgeous sea change after all.

Alas, several more detours lay in wait! Rick secured a job in Townsville. However, when he went to collect his uniform HR told him he didn't have a job. He had mentioned on his application that he *might* have occupational hearing loss. The company had undertaken hearing tests as part of Rick's medical, which showed no evidence of hearing loss. Despite this, they refused to employ him.

Our 'adventures,' let's call them that, took us inland to Charters Towers. Rick secured another job and was told he would have to wait two weeks to commence. By this time we were feeling unsettled, to say the least, and wanted to put down some roots. The employment officer in Charters Towers told Rick Mount Isa would be the best place to secure a job immediately. We hit the road yet again, travelling further and further inland. The further we went, the hotter it became.

We arrived in Mount Isa to discover we were literally in outback Australia. Red dust aside, Mount Isa is a fascinating city. What began as a humble mining town is now among the top 10 producers of copper, zinc, lead and silver. It attracts thousands of tourists each year for its wildlife, rugged outback and scenic lakes.

We were fortunate that Rick secured a job as a fitter and turner the same day we arrived. I desperately wanted the girls to have stability after so long. I was excited that we would have our own family home again.

Bam...another detour. There was a housing shortage in the popular mining town, and we were informed that the only accommodation available was a caravan in a camping ground. Frankly, I'd had enough of cars, motels, cabins, caravans, or anything related to camping. I just wanted our young family to be settled and live in a proper home again.

It was then I recalled the picture I had received in New Zealand at prayer group - the map of Australia with a dot towards the top right-hand side. *I realised we had ended up in the place I had seen on the map!* We were on the right track after all, albeit a dusty one.

Living in the caravan was fun. We made friends with other families in the park and the girls had on-demand friends every day. After a few months we decided it would be nice to buy our own caravan.

Bang...yet another detour. Mount Isa not only had a housing shortage, it also had a caravan shortage. I searched for weeks on end with Phil, one of our cheery neighbours in the caravan park. Because Rick was usually out of town working Phil sometimes accompanied the girls and I on our daily van search. However, any caravans I liked were occupied, old, rusty, or too small for our family.

Driving through our van park one day, I slowed down to negotiate a speed bump. One of the caravans caught my eye. I slammed the **Frustration** button on my walkie talkie, and I slammed it again just for good measure: "God that one would be perfect; right size, not too old, no rust and towable." I cried out, "God, please, I would love one just like that." It was a tiny house with an enclosed private yard and children's swings. The **Frustration** button certainly had some use that day.

Later, when chatting with Phil, I told him I had found the perfect caravan but it was not for sale. He simply stated, "Why don't you ask them if they would like to sell it?" I did not want to look foolish and did not follow up on his idea. Phil returned later that evening. He told me he had spoken to the owners of the lovely caravan and - they did not want to sell and had no intention of moving. This was all too much. Rick and I and our two small girls desperately needed a home.

A loud knock woke me the next morning. Phil was standing at our door, grinning broadly. "You're not going to believe this. The van owners have changed their minds overnight. They have decided to leave Mount Isa and they want to sell you the caravan!"

The tiny van was the perfect home for us with built-in bunk beds for the girls, toys, a barbecue, and a fully fenced yard. Our girls loved their tiny house and tiny yard and we created many fond memories during the following year. This style of living was to impact me for the rest of my life. It birthed within me a newfound appreciation of nature and the outdoors. All these years later, my preference is to watch the wonders of the night sky rather than TV.

On our journey we encountered many detours that seemed to throw us off course. In hindsight, they were just part of our journey.

We could not have orchestrated the circumstances that led us to Mount Isa but God knew all along that's where we would end up! I was astounded at God's ingenuity and creativity. That simple picture, given months beforehand, gave me much needed reassurance at a very uncertain time in my life.

The literal speed bump in the van park was a great lesson. If I had not slowed down, at that precise moment, I would not have seen the van that became our tiny home. I had driven over that speed bump so often, but this time I slowed down enough to observe my surroundings. We often see detours and speed bumps as a hindrance, but sometimes God uses them to slow us down and take notice. He may be trying to speak to us or want us to change direction.

God also provided reassurance and direction ahead of time. He knew exactly where we would end up, even though that was not our intended destination. All the incongruous junctions we encountered were simply detours that would lead us to our destination.

Detours can change our lives for the better even though they can seem inconvenient at the time. It is reassuring to know that ultimately God controls our destiny if we allow Him to do so.

> P.S. I didn't have one asthma attack during our time in Mount Isa.

Have you reached a major detour in your life? Warning signs with flashing lights may be blinding you. The road may be filled with potholes. You might be tempted to set up camp in one of those potholes and throw a pity-party-for-one.

If this is you, God has an important message:

Don't spend your life in a pothole

You may also want to read about Joseph, in GENESIS 37-47, and the many detours he encountered. His story is inspiring because many people, including his family, were against him but He continued to trust God. He went from the pit to the palace but had many detours along the way.

CHAPTER EIGHT

JOURNAL THE JOURNEY

The next leg of our journey led us back to Townsville, in North Queensland Australia, where Rick had secured work. I decided to keep track of our journey and started jotting a few notes here and there mainly about the girls' schooling and other activities. My notes were more like morse code - only I could decipher the hieroglyphics. As mentioned, writing is not my strong point and I had no intention of sharing my reflections with anybody.

I was having a walkie talkie time one day when I felt the familiar nudge of the Holy Spirit and heard Him whisper, **"I want you to journal the journey."** I laughed, telling myself the walkie talkie had a crossed signal. This was clearly meant for someone else. Again, I heard, **"I want you to journal the journey."**

My mind raced through the tunnel of past failures like an express train hauling carriage after carriage of writing blunders. I know I have strengths but writing isn't one of them. Have I mentioned that? It was then I began to have a fresh appreciation of how Moses felt when God asked him to lead His people out of Egypt - well, perhaps on a lesser scale.

Moses had a speech impediment and feared public speaking. I thought it only reasonable that I respond like Moses so I began to state my case. "Father, I am no writer. You know I missed so much school due to having asthma as a child. You know how frustrated I get trying to express myself." I was on a roll. "I am also a great procrastinator which is not entirely my fault. You must have made me that way."

I felt that God understood my excuses and reasoning. He just listened as I expressed my fears, feelings, and failures. However, in the days ahead I would discover that God was to have the last say. His plan was simple and He wasted no time confirming that He wanted me to journal my journey.

Rick and I were going on a holiday to our homeland, New Zealand. Our trip included a stopover at a friend's place on the Gold Coast. I was only there 10 minutes when my friend, Lisa, announced she had a small gift for me. She was also quick to admit she had purchased the gift for herself, but felt God wanted me to have it. As I took the gift I recall thinking it felt like a book.

When I opened the gift I discovered it was indeed a book. However, the only word in the entire book was emblazoned on the front cover in large letters, *JOURNAL*. As I held the journal in my hand I knew this was no coincidence. I was amazed that God would confirm He wanted me to journal the journey. The lines had not been crossed after all and the initial walkie talkie message had been correct. As I packed my new journal in my suitcase I told myself there would be no more procrastination.

On the second week of my holiday, while visiting friends in Tauranga, I was in the kitchen helping my friend's daughter, Keryn, cook tea. Those of you who know me will realise this is a stretch. I don't know what I like least, writing or cooking. I did say I was 'helping' so interpret that as you will. We were having a good old natter when Keryn stopped cooking and said, "Jenni, you need to journal." I was speechless, another thing which does not often happen.

Over dinner I shared with my friend, her husband, and their daughter about my walkie talkie time and how God had told me to journal the journey. I also told them about receiving a brand-new journal as a gift. We joked about God having to making it extra obvious due to me being blonde and having the gift of procrastination.

The following morning my friends and I headed off to church. The guest preacher stood to announce she wasn't going to preach the sermon she had prepared. She felt God wanted her to preach about a different topic. Her new sermon topic: *Journal the Journey*.

My friends and I stifled laughter. It was incredibly faith-building for us to witness God's ongoing nagging (I mean encouragement) for me to journal.

> **Then the Lord said to me, "Write my answer plainly on tablets, so that a runner can carry the correct message to others."**
> HABAKKUK 2:2 - TLB

God knew how much I struggled with writing and how much I procrastinate. He knew I needed an extra boost to get me moving and He was happy to send walkie talkie messages via other people to confirm what he had originally spoken to me. I know I would not have written this book if God had not spoken through others to encourage me to journal.

Life can be hectic at times. If, like me, you have the gift of procrastination it can be doubly challenging to put pen to paper. Finding a type of journaling that suits you can make all the difference. If you're not keen on traditional journaling you might prefer to think outside the box and try some of the ideas on the next page. And, whatever form of journaling you use, remember it's always more fun when it's a two-way conversation.

> **Jot down words or phrases during the day;**
> **Write down, sing, or meditate on Bible verses;**
> **Write down the words of your favourite songs;**
> **Jot down prayers and God's responses;**
> **Use a recording app for two-way conversations;**
> **Be creative with: art, poetry, music, craft;**
> **There's no right or wrong way to journal.**

CHAPTER NINE

TRUST AND OBEY

During a walkie talkie time in 2010 the old hymn *Trust and Obey* popped into my mind. I had learned enough to know this was not a coincidence, but another one of those God-incidences. What was God's message for me? He was asking me to trust Him in every area of my life. The message was timely as I would soon be heading to Melbourne Bible College to study a Certificate IV in Ministry. I would not have a regular income while studying and felt God wanted me to trust Him to provide for me financially.

Initially, I wondered if God would settle for me crooning the words to the hymn *Trust and Obey* instead of applying it practically. However, when I made the choice to trust God I found it surprisingly easy to take this message to heart. I was excited to see how He would provide for me. I also had an overwhelming sense of peace like I had experienced at ladies group all those years ago. The peace was like a friendly nudge from God, **"You can trust me. I really will look after you."** I also had savings, and was good at budgeting, so I was doing my part as well. I knew I had to be thrifty with the money I had.

About a month into my studies several well-meaning and caring friends suggested I apply for study allowance. On a logical level I knew this made sense, so during another walkie talkie time I told God I was changing my mind and would apply for Austudy. I applied and immediately lost that wonderful sense of peace. Several weeks after applying, a young man from Centrelink phoned and asked if I could go into the centre. He told me my application had been rejected. He seemed shocked and said he would like to help me appeal the decision. I knew God was giving me a second chance to trust Him and I politely declined the young man's offer. The following Bible verse jumped out at me during a walkie talkie time and I knew God was again reassuring me. It was like a handwritten note addressed to *Jen-Jen*.

> **THEREFORE I TELL YOU, DO NOT WORRY ABOUT YOUR LIFE, WHAT YOU WILL EAT OR DRINK; OR ABOUT YOUR BODY, WHAT YOU WILL WEAR. IS NOT LIFE MORE THAN FOOD, AND THE BODY MORE THAN CLOTHES? LOOK AT THE BIRDS OF THE AIR; THEY DO NOT SOW OR REAP OR STORE AWAY IN BARNS, AND YET YOUR HEAVENLY FATHER FEEDS THEM. ARE YOU NOT MUCH MORE VALUABLE THAN THEY? CAN ANY ONE OF YOU BY WORRYING ADD A SINGLE HOUR TO YOUR LIFE? AND WHY DO YOU WORRY ABOUT CLOTHES? SEE HOW THE FLOWERS OF THE FIELD GROW. THEY DO NOT LABOUR OR SPIN. YET I TELL YOU THAT NOT EVEN SOLOMON IN ALL HIS SPLENDOUR WAS DRESSED LIKE ONE OF THESE. IF THAT IS HOW**

> **GOD CLOTHES THE GRASS OF THE FIELD, WHICH IS HERE TODAY AND TOMORROW IS THROWN INTO THE FIRE, WILL HE NOT MUCH MORE CLOTHE YOU - YOU OF LITTLE FAITH? SO DO NOT WORRY, SAYING, 'WHAT SHALL WE EAT?' OR 'WHAT SHALL WE DRINK?' OR 'WHAT SHALL WE WEAR?'**
> MATTHEW 6:25-30 - NIV

I was to learn my first lesson during a Melbourne winter. A North Queensland winter wardrobe consists of a jumper and a pair of jeans. I was not prepared for a Melbourne winter; no warm coat, winter boots, or even a pair of closed-in shoes. I realised my only option was to find a second-hand store and buy some winter gear. I was not sold on the idea but soon realised I would have to change my attitude. A change in attitude may seem inconsequential. However, I have discovered it can be a powerful precursor for allowing God to work.

I was really struggling to change my attitude until I had a light bulb moment. I recalled Jan, a close friend of mine. She has a knack for discovering brand-name clothing in second-hand stores. She always looks amazing and has some fabulous outfits. I told myself I needed to have a Jan mentality and not a Jen mentality when it came to shopping for winter clothes. The acronym WWJD? had its meaning slightly altered to *What would Jan do?*

With my *WWJD* mantra guiding me it did not take long to find my favourite second-hand store. This shop always had something perfect for me, like my brand-new winter boots. I would regularly find new stylish clothes, books that were perfect for Bible College studies, and other knick-knacks. I often received compliments for my fashion sense and people asked where I shopped. Shopping at second-hand stores had become a satisfying and wonderful adventure.

One chilly winter's day I was shopping and unable to find anything. I decided to leave empty-handed. As the door closed behind me my walkie talkie clicked. I almost ignored it but decided to tune in. I heard that still small voice I know so well, **"Go back into the shop."** I replied, "You must be kidding. I have just spent an hour there. There is nothing in there for me today!" The voice persisted, **"Go over to the counter."** I stood at the counter feeling like a goose, muttering under my breath, "Well, here I am!" **"Look in the glass cabinet."** Looking back at me was a tiny, delicate 9-carat gold ring. As I leaned forward, to get a closer look, I noticed the price tag - $25. 00. *Wow, that's cheap*, I thought.

I asked the sales assistant if I could try it on. She said in a condescending tone, "I've had numerous women try that ring, but it has an exceedingly small band. I don't like your chances." Her manner made me nervous and I had to agree it was certainly a tiny ring. *No wonder it's so cheap*, I reasoned. As it slid effortlessly onto my finger I heard the familiar voice, **"See, I told you."** The shop assistant stumbled over her words, "So many women have tried on that ring. I cannot believe it fits you!"

My 9-carat gold ring had two overlapping hearts: one large heart with a smaller heart linked below. The message was clear; God's heart and mine were linked forever. His heart was so much larger than mine and He was able to care for and provide for me in ways I could never imagine. If I had not trusted Him, and obeyed his unusual message, I would have forfeited the lifelong symbolic message the ring would always have for me.

God provided above and beyond what I could have imagined during those 12 months. The clothes and ring were just a small part of His provision. He also provided a castle for me to live in - literally, a house like a castle. When I first arrived in Melbourne I was renting a tiny room for $100 a week. Thanks to some amazing God-incidences I ended up living in a house like a castle – it literally had turrets! Some of its other features included; a tennis court, marble tiles, an art studio, and the fact I didn't have to pay a cent more than I had at the previous residence. I thank God for His provision that year. It still puts a smile on my face when I think of all the blessings I received just because I trusted Him to look after me.

Sometimes the most logical route is not the one God wants us to take. It made perfect sense to apply for Austudy, absolutely perfect sense. The thing about faith is you can't really explain it to someone else. It often doesn't make sense to them. That's when knowing God's voice is so important. And the path He tells me to take could be completely different from the path He tells you to take.

Doing what you think God is telling you to do often takes courage. God may be saying to you, **"Be strong and courageous."**

> **Be strong and very courageous. Be careful to obey all the law my servant Moses gave to you; do not turn from it to the right or to the left, that you may be successful wherever you go.**
> Joshua 1:7 - NIV

Chapter Ten

THAT SOUNDS FISHY

Just another day at Bible College in Melbourne. The class discussion was around temple tax. In short, this was a tax required of Jewish males, over the age of 20, and the money was used for upkeep and maintenance of the temple. You would think Jesus would be exempt from forking out money towards this, right? Wrong. If you want to read the whole story go to MATTHEW 17:24-27.

The condensed version is that to avoid scandal or controversy Jesus agreed to pay temple tax for Peter, his Disciple, and himself. Jesus produced a novel way of acquiring the money. He instructed Peter to pull a coin from the mouth of a fish, a little fish swimming in the ocean minding its own business.

While the rest of the class discussion focused on the controversy of paying taxes and exemptions my mind wandered, as it often does, to the more practical aspects. I was mulling over the words of Jesus to Peter.

> **Go to the sea, drop in a hook, and take the first fish that comes up. Open its mouth and you will find a coin worth twice the temple tax. Give that to them for me and for you.**
> MATTHEW 17:27 - NIV

Generous, I thought. Jesus was thinking not only of himself, but also Peter.

Then I started thinking, what did Peter think when Jesus sent him on this curious fishing expedition? I imagine Peter, being a seasoned fisherman, may have scratched his head a little over this odd request. "Sorry, I must have misheard you, Jesus. I'm going fishing for money, not fish? Fish don't generally come to the surface with a two-drachma coin sitting in their mouth." Then I imagined Peter's mind whirling as he retorted, "Hang on, have I been fishing for the wrong type of fish? Is there actually an ocean full of fish out there with coins in their mouths? I've been doing this fishing gig the wrong way for years!" I imagined Peter and Jesus both having a good chuckle at Peter's response.

On that chilly winter's evening, as I drove home from Bible College, my thoughts were consumed with this story. I pressed the **Doubt** button on my walkie talkie. "Lord, you know I've heard every fishing story there is, but this is the story to end all fishing stories. How did you arrange for the coin to be in the mouth of a fish? Did the fish search for it in the depths of the ocean? Did a fisherman drop it overboard while the fish waited below? Did it appear out of thin air?"

Despite my questions I also saw the funny side of the story. I could picture Jesus standing there with a huge smirk on His face winking at Peter as he told him to go fishing for a coin. I chuckled to myself. How clever Jesus was to use the very profession Peter knew best to bamboozle him, whilst simultaneously meeting a need.

I arrived home totally exhausted. I climbed the long, winding staircase, plonking one foot in front of the other. I dropped my books and laptop on the bench and slid down the wall to the floor. I felt warm and cozy as I listened to the howling wind outside.

Just as I was starting to relax the walkie talkie whirred and I heard that wee inner voice I have come to know so well, **"Go downstairs to the car."** "You have to be kidding me," I retorted. Moments later, I heard it again,

"Go down to the car." I sighed, dragged myself up the wall and trudged down all those stairs into the frosty night air. My attitude towards God matched the weather, cold and bitter.

Impatiently I sighed, "Now what?" **"Lift up the mat in the front passenger side of your car."** I lifted the mat on the passenger side of the car and laughed out loud. There, under the mat, smack-bang in the middle, was a one-dollar coin! To this day I still have no idea how it got there.

WALKIE TALKIE FAITH

One of my life philosophies is: *If in doubt, check it out!* I certainly had some doubts about how Peter could go fishing and catch a *Coin Fish*. Because of my heart-to-heart relationship with God, I knew it was fine to question him about this fishy scenario. I popped on my *Inquisitive Inquirer* hat and had a chat with Him. God responded to my honesty in a way I didn't expect. I still have no idea how the coin came to be under the mat.

You may think finding a coin under a car mat is nothing to write home about. You may also wonder if this was simply a coincidence rather than a God-incidence. However, the true significance lay in what the coin symbolised for me. Remember, that very morning, I had queried how a coin came to be in the mouth of a fish and God answered me by letting me find a coin! I definitely saw His sense of humour in this situation.

If you are keeping your distance from God because you think your doubts are wrong think again. God's love is unconditional. He welcomes your doubts, fears, struggles, and concerns. He has extremely broad shoulders and is certainly willing and able to deal with your questions and doubts. He would rather hear your doubts than not hear from you at all.

Many people in the Bible expressed their doubts. Just two doubters were Habakkuk and Thomas. Habakkuk even shouted at God.

> "How long, oh God, must I call for help but you do not listen?"
> HABAKKUK 1:1-3 - NIV

Chapter Eleven

My Moses Speech

I always think it's a great idea to maintain some semblance of sanity; well, as much as one can. God clearly wanted to challenge this, and I wanted to challenge Him right back. One day I had an odd thought. God was on the walkie talkie trying to get my attention.

God's idea was that I contact one of my ex-tutors from the Bible College I had attended in Melbourne and give her a message. I was to tell her, "Go ahead with the book you are intending to write." My well-worn catchphrase spilled from my lips, "You've got to be kidding me?" God continued to pester me (I mean lay an impression on my heart) to contact her and tell her she was to write a book. Again, my response was, "You must be kidding me, God. How do I know if she's even contemplating writing a book?" *Silence...*

I knew this was one of those times where God had already spoken and was not inclined to repeat Himself. It was faith versus reason time. I wondered if there was a sneaky way I could discover if she was writing a book but, alas, sneakiness eluded me. I didn't even have her phone number to casually point the conversation in that direction. Fortunately, or unfortunately for me, I did have her email address.

Immediately, I did what any good Christian would do. I rang a friend and went for coffee. I knew I had a good reason for not emailing her; I did not want to look foolish. Secretly, I hoped God would change His mind and graciously announce, **"Jen, Jen, it's okay. You don't have to do it. How about you pray for her instead?"**

The longer I delayed the sicker I felt. However, I had one last trick up my exceedingly long sleeve of tricks. When all else fails resort to the Moses speech. I have to say I really did myself proud. I stated my case like an overly enthusiastic defence lawyer. "Godddddd," I pleaded, "Surely you can find someone else to do this, someone who is adept at writing? I have a few people in mind I can direct you to. Goddddd, are you sure you don't want to find someone else? I mean, I don't want you to look bad after all. I'm only thinking of you in all this, can't you see? You know writing is not my strong point, or perhaps you have forgotten? It would be better for all concerned if you asked someone else; well really, anyone but me, Lord."

God didn't seem too taken with my eloquent speech. In fact, He seemed to ignore it. The walkie talkie remained silent. I realised that meant He did not have anyone else in mind for this assignment. Despite feeling like a dill, I decided to step out in faith. I wanted to please God and I knew how important faith was to Him.

I eventually emailed my tutor and delivered the strange message. I didn't know if I would ever hear back from her. Or perhaps I would receive an email along the lines of, "Um, I think you've got your wires crossed, Jenni. Did you mean to send this email to someone else?"

Not long after sending the email I received a response. She told me she had been putting off writing a challenging book and had been asking for direction. My email was exactly what she needed. It gave her the courage to write the book.

The following year I received a complimentary copy of her book. I was stunned when reading the title, *The Morning after Suicide*. It was only then, with tears streaming down my face, I realised why God had chosen little old me for this assignment. I had also lost someone very close to suicide.

> **For just as the heavens are higher than the earth, so are my ways higher than yours, and my thoughts than yours.**
> **ISAIAH 55:9 – NIV**

I am incredibly grateful God knows me better than I know myself. His love, understanding and patience constantly astound me. Because He knows me through and through He knew how I would respond to His request. He also knew I would eventually step out, even at the risk of being wrong, or appearing foolish.

I imagine Him having a chuckle as He pressed the **_Special Assignment_** button on his walkie talkie. He knew it would take me three weeks to deftly weave my excuses into an impressive _Excuses Rug_. He also knew I would eventually release the threads and disentangle my creation.

I learned, yet again, as with any walkie talkie message, the Gold Standard of Authenticity remains:

> Is it in keeping with the Bible's principles?

> Will it edify and encourage the receiver?

Does God have a ***Special Assignment*** for you? Special Assignments can be small, large, or in between. They can be grand and life-changing or seemingly insignificant. Never under-estimate the blessing you can be in someone's life.

Chapter Twelve

GIVE ME A SIGN

As mentioned, I was born and raised in New Zealand. My parents built their first home in New Zealand shortly after they were married and lived there for nearly 60 years. I lived at home until I was 19 when I left to marry Rick. Mum and dad were very crafty - in the nicest possible way. Dad made wooden pens and fruit bowls. Mum created inspiring cards and other knick-knacks. My family had an in-joke that mum couldn't wait for us to fly the coop so she could convert yet another bedroom into a craft room.

As mum and dad aged, and their health declined, they needed to sell the family home and move into a retirement village. I returned to New Zealand for six weeks to spend time with them and help them move. Remember the wonderful home-made crafts and knick-knacks? Deciding what to do with a lifetime of treasures, each holding a special memory, was incredibly difficult emotionally and logistically for mum, dad, and myself. It was heartbreaking and harrowing.

I decided to take a break and give mum and dad a break. A friend of mine in New Zealand had mentioned several retreats that were being held on a remote island in New Zealand. I decided to attend one. I narrowed down my choice to three possibilities: *The Father Heart of God*, *The Shack*, and *End Times*. The *Father Heart of God* appealed to me, but I decided to pray about it first. I hit the **Question** button on my walkie talkie. After all, if I was going to a retreat to spend time with God it made sense I should ask Him which one would be most suitable.

The following day, during a worship time at church, I had a picture pop into my mind. God was on the walkie talkie again. The image was so clear it looked like a painting on the church wall. I had absolutely no idea what it meant, or how it related to me. It was a picture of an old derelict cabin.

Soon after, I went shopping and happened to park near a new billboard. As I exited my car I couldn't help but see the large billboard. It was advertising a new coffee shop called *The Shack*. I recalled my prayer about which retreat to attend and realised that God was literally giving me a sign. I laughed thinking God needed to make the sign so obvious because I was blonde. I had also learned not to assume. I wanted to ensure this was a God-incidence rather than a coincidence.

I hastily finished my shopping and rushed home to investigate *The Shack* retreat on the internet. My first thought was, *If I attend a retreat about a book will I actually have to read the book?* As I Googled details of the retreat I hoped to find a proviso stating, "Retreat attendees should not read the book under any circumstances."

In the midst of my Googling I stumbled upon *The Shack* book cover and almost fell off my chair. The cover was identical to the vision I had seen in church - the old derelict cabin!

I was amazed God had spoken to me in such a creative way. He was obviously happy to confirm which retreat to attend. The internet, a vision on the wall of a church, and a carpark billboard were His novel ways of letting me know.

I reflected on the many ways God had spoken to people in the Bible; too many to mention. Here are just a few: An Angel spoke to Mary telling her she would be the mother of Jesus; a star guided the Wise Men to Jesus at his birth; the Wise Men were warned in a dream not to return to Herod - a dream that ultimately saved their lives. God uses such unexpected and novel ways to communicate with us.

Are you set in your ways and views about how God can speak to you? It may benefit you to press the **Refresh** button on your walkie talkie. Who knows what new adventures await?

Chapter Thirteen

FRIDAY NIGHT AT THE SERVO

Allow me to set the scene: It was Friday night at the servo. I know, I know, excitement to the max. I was going about my business, putting petrol in my car, as one tends to do at a service station. I noticed a tall man putting petrol in a brown van. I found my mind ticking over like the petrol bowser, thinking random thoughts. It was then I decided to call him Brown Van Man (BVM). It was all pretty much to be expected, a nothing-to-see-here type moment, just a mundane Friday night at the servo, or so I thought.

While filling my car I felt the familiar click of the walkie talkie. God was prompting me to bless BVM by paying for his fuel. *There goes the ho-hum Friday night at the servo* I thought. *Gee, thanks, God.*

Awkward does not cover how I felt. I stood there trying to figure out how I could do this without appearing foolish. I proudly came up with several brilliant solutions: jump in my car and drive away as quickly as possible; drive past BVM, roll down my window and throw the money at him; hand the money directly to the service station owner to pay for BVM's fuel; walk up to Brown Van Man and say, "Hey, I feel like God told me to give you this money."

By the time I had finished arguing with God, and creating my four-point plan, BVM had driven off. I was left standing there, petrol pump in hand, mouth open like a clown at a fair. I clearly knew what God had wanted me to do, but I had let fear of embarrassment prevent me from blessing BVM.

As I drove away, I had to pull over to the side of the road to dry my tears. I had prevented BVM from receiving a blessing simply because I was concerned I would look foolish. I pressed the **Remorse** button on my walkie talkie. Amidst tears and sobs I pleaded, "Please, please give me a second chance. I'm so sorry. Please give me another chance."

I regularly visited the service station hoping I would see Brown Van Man again, especially after my remorseful walkie talkie prayer. I was determined to follow through this time. Much to my disappointment weeks turned to months and months turned to years without so much as a glimpse of BVM.

Two years later I attended a Prophetic Conference at a church in Townsville. There were 150 people in attendance and I did not know a soul. We were asked to pair up with someone we didn't know, easily done. I found myself standing in front of a very tall man with broad shoulders. As this was a Prophets Conference we were to ask God to give us a message for the person we had partnered with, no matter how seemingly insignificant it may seem.

As I clicked my walkie talkie button I asked God to give me a message for this man. The response was not so much a message as a question: **"Ask this guy if he drives a Tarago."** Unfiltered thoughts: *God you've got to be kidding me! I'm not asking that. Why would you want me to ask him that?*

Because we were in a friendly setting, where we were learning to receive messages from God, I thought I would take the plunge. With my head bowed and my eyes closed I took a deep breath and asked the man, "Do you own a Tarago?" I held my breath waiting for his baffled response. He replied, "Yes, I do. How do you know that?" I told him God had just told me. I then heard the familiar sound of the walkie talkie: **"This is Brown Van Man from the service station two years ago."**

I almost had to pick myself up off the floor. I managed to compose myself before asking him if he ever bought petrol for his van at my local station. He told me that he used his brown van to collect people who did not have transport to attend church activities and, yes, there had been times when he purchased fuel from that service station. He went on to mention at times he did not have enough money to put petrol in the van. He said he drove around on the smell of an oily rag and relied on the grace of God to provide money for fuel. It was all starting to make sense.

Without a word I left Brown Van Man and darted away like an Olympic athlete. He had no idea where I was going, but I was in a hurry to keep my promise to God. As quickly as I could, I returned and gave him the original amount of money, along with two years' interest.

I learned several lessons from my Friday night at the Servo. Firstly, I had remained expectant. I believed I would see BVM again and be able to bless him as God intended. In fact, for two years, I returned to the servo many Friday nights hoping to see him.

Secondly, I was genuinely sorry, not simply on a surface level but on a heart level. You may think what I did, or didn't do, wasn't a big deal but it was to me. My fear of looking foolish stopped me from blessing someone. I was reminded of Jonah running from God and the second chance God gave him. I was incredibly grateful for second chances.

God meets our needs in ways we could never anticipate or orchestrate. What a brilliant plan He devised to allow me to see BVM again. I assumed I would run into him at the servo, thus my frequent visits. God's ways are so different to our ways. He will continually surprise us if we tune into His plans.

Have you given up on yourself? Do you think you are beyond God's reach? No matter what you have done God is waiting to forgive you. If you are truly sorry He will give you a second chance. He is a God of countless chances.

> **But if we confess our sins to Him He can be depended on to forgive us and to cleanse us from every wrong. And it is perfectly proper for God to do this for us because Christ died to wash away our sins.** *I JOHN 1:9 - TLB*

PART 2

WALKIE TALKIE FAITH

DURING TRAGEDY

Chapter Fourteen

THE BLUE TARPAULIN

It was 3:00 am Boxing Day morning, the year was 2006. I was mind-numbingly exhausted, but sleep was impossible. Slumped on the curb across the road from our family home I surveyed the most horrific scene imaginable. Surely this was a nightmare and I would soon awaken? Blood rushed through my veins. My heart took on its own fast, furious, contorted rhythm. A chilling sense of shock stood like a steel barrier preventing tears from falling. This was perhaps a blessing; if I had started crying an ocean of tears would have ensued.

The air was filled with the overpowering stench of smoke from the fire that had engulfed our family home. The sound of exploding glass continuously rang in my ears. The *Crime Scene* barrier seemed oddly out of place emblazoned around the perimeter of our family home. A Police Officer was assigned the task of ensuring nobody tampered with potential evidence until the Forensic Team arrived. I imbibed the scene in disbelief.

Prior to this unfathomable event I was at my daughter's house relaxing, watching a movie. It was approximately 8. 30 pm when the phone rang.

Little did I know that phone call was to change our lives forever. Panic rose in my daughter's voice as she relayed the information. "Mum, we have to go right now! There's a fire at your place. " The five-minute drive to our family home seemed like an eternity. What on earth had happened?

When we arrived, there were several bystanders and neighbours outside the house frozen like garden statues. Fire was engulfing our home. My daughter's words of desperation echoed in the night air, "Has anyone seen my father? Has anyone seen my father?" It was then I realised Rick was nowhere in sight.

I panicked, thinking he was probably asleep in the games room which was not yet ablaze. I pictured him sleeping peacefully, snoring in front of the TV as he often did. A thousand thoughts tumbled through my mind, the most pressing of them being that I must save Rick. I could not bear the thought of him burning in the blaze. There was an adjoining fence blocking access to the games room. I asked two male bystanders to help me push down the fence. The sense of urgency caused adrenaline to surge through our bodies, resulting in a Hulk-like strength which allowed us to demolish the fence.

As the fence came tumbling down, little did I know so would my world. Nothing could have prepared me for what I was about to see - there in front of me was Rick's lifeless body. My knees buckled and I fell to the ground. I was unable to comprehend the scene before me. Had Rick started the fire and taken his own life?

Time stood still for the next six hours. I kept trying to absorb the reality of what had happened. Frozen in shock, all I could do was stare at a blue tarpaulin which, by that time, had been placed amidst the rubble in the front yard. With a pounding heart I waited anxiously for the tarp to move.

I waited for the slightest movement, any sort of movement. I knew the blue tarpaulin covering Rick's body would never move, not even an inch.

There are no words to describe the disbelief, shock, and heartache I felt for myself and our two girls. I wondered how my girls would go on after what their father had done. My brain felt like slush as I struggled to comprehend the evening's events. One word reverberated loudly and incessantly. Why? Why? Why? It was implausible that my once strong, rational, level-headed husband started the fire that destroyed our family home and then took his own life. Regardless, my heart ached for Rick. I could not contemplate leaving him alone under the blue tarpaulin. I kept thinking, *I cannot leave. I cannot leave Rick alone under the blue tarpaulin.*

The sun rose brightly, oblivious to my plight. As dawn broke, I felt the comforting arm of my brother envelop me, telling me it was time to leave. He could see how exhausted I was, mentally, physically, emotionally. He assured me the Police Officer would take care of Rick. Although I knew he was right, I struggled to leave and the same thoughts plagued me. *I cannot leave Rick. I cannot leave him here alone.* Eventually I had to leave. I turned to survey the scene, a scene that would be forever etched in my mind - the motionless blue tarpaulin amidst a sea of ash.

As I walked away with the comforting arm of my brother supporting me, I heard my walkie talkie click. Even then, even in the midst of my most debilitating pain, God was there. **"I know what you are going through**

and although I cannot be with you in person my Spirit will never leave you." An unexpected sense of peace enveloped me.

Even amidst my crushing pain I saw God's provision and blessing. The one person in the world I would have chosen to be with me was there, providing support and comfort. My brother had not spent Christmas with us before as he lives in New Zealand. An unusual set of circumstances had brought him across the Tasman that year. I asked myself, *Is this a coincidence or a God-incidence?*

Hopefully, nobody will experience what I did on that Christmas day in 2006 and in the months and years that followed. Sadly, I know suffering is part of life and many of you have experienced suffering of your own. We can rest assured that Jesus truly understands. He experienced deep suffering, pain, and sorrow in His life. He understood what I was going through and He understands what you are going through no matter how deep and dark your pain may feel. Jesus clearly knew the pain of grief when He said:

> **"My soul is crushed with grief to the point of death."**
> MARK 14:34 - NLT

This story has been changed countless times. A regular conversation between Madonna (my ghostwriter, not the singer) and I went something along these lines: Jen: "I'm still not happy with one of the stories." Madonna: "The Blue Tarpaulin?" I now realise, regardless of how much time we spent poring over the contents, I would never be able to convey the depth of heartbreak and anguish I experienced that night and during the following months.

I also realised that some tragedies are so life-changing there will never be satisfactory answers or a clear resolution. I knew I needed to make a choice if my future was going to have any meaning whatsoever. Whether I acknowledged it or not I was making a choice to *Rely or Run*. I could rely on God or run from Him. God has given me free-will and I could have justifiably clung to bitterness and anger. I decided this was not a time to run from God, but to run to Him. I chose to allow God to take my hand and comfort me. In doing so I realised I still had so much life to live and so much to give, even after such a life-altering tragedy. You would not be reading this book if I had chosen to run from God.

Chapter Fifteen

A NEEDLE IN A HAYSTACK

Only those who have lost a loved one to suicide can understand its complexity. Those left behind struggle to make sense of something utterly incomprehensible. Trying to find a reasonable answer to the question "Why?" was akin to looking for a needle in a haystack.

A torrent of questions pummelled my mind relentlessly, like a fierce ocean smashing against an outcrop of jagged rocks. These also gave rise to a tide of emotion that dragged me unwillingly out to sea. I felt like a tiny, fragile boat in the midst of a cyclone.

What didn't help was my inability to fit the pieces of the puzzle together. I desperately searched for answers the week after Rick's death, but my mind was a blur. My recollection of that horrendous night is fragmented and vague, which has been a blessing. I spent countless minutes, hours, days, weeks, and months wondering what had been going on in Rick's mind prior to his death. Friends and family also racked their brains to see if there were any telltale signs we may have missed. Finally, we came up with several possible red flags:

Rick had recently started to despise the phone: speaking on it; hearing me speak on it; he could not even bear to hear it ring.

In recent years he no longer wanted to work full-time, which was totally out of character for him. He had always prided himself on being a hard worker and loved taking on new challenges and projects.

In the months leading up to his death he contracted a rare, tropical infection which began as an ear infection but eventually spread further, causing his brain to swell. Had this infection affected his brain and his ability to think rationally?

Rick and Scotch didn't mix well – at all. It affected him so badly I decided there was a good reason Scotch is called a spirit. For this reason he had not consumed it for several years. After the fire I was talking to a friend who had kindly moved our rubbish bin out of the fire's range. He told me a neighbour had recently given Rick a bottle of Scotch as a thank-you gift for work Rick had done during the year.

Again, searching for the proverbial needle in the haystack, we decided to investigate. We approached the bin gingerly and flipped the lid to discover not just one, but two empty bottles of Scotch. This gave rise to more questions: Why did he drink it? Why did he drink alone? When did he drink it? Did he drink two bottles in one sitting?

Rick had clearly not been coping and I wondered if the red flags were all pointing towards clinical depression. Rick certainly had many symptoms of depression: brain fog, difficulty concentrating, forgetfulness, inability to cope with everyday tasks, anger outbursts in response to the smallest requests. Perhaps he could have received help if we had recognised the signs earlier.

During this time, my walkie talkie faith was sorely tested. After months of questioning, and not receiving answers, I realised I would never know what happened on that fateful evening, or whether I would have been able to prevent it.

I didn't find a needle. I didn't even find a haystack! However, I did find a God I could trust. The clearest walkie talkie message I received during my needle search was not, **"The needle is over there. There is your answer,"** but instead, **"Just trust me no matter what."**

> **Trust in the Lord with all your heart and lean not on your own understanding; in all your ways submit to him, and he will make your paths straight.** PROVERBS 3:4-6 - NIV

As I searched for answers I was surprised to see the Bible mentioned suicide. This provided me with an amazing amount of comfort. I imagined those grieving friends and families left behind, just like me, with no clear answers either. I no longer felt so alone.

After much soul-searching and all the "Why God?" questions I realised nobody can ever understand why a loved one makes the choice to take their life. Only God knows what is in a person's heart PSALM 139:1-2. He knows the depth of pain that brings someone to the point of suicide.

This Bible verse gave me hope and reminded me how all-encompassing God's love is. The Apostle Paul makes it clear that nothing can separate us from God's love:

> **And I am convinced that nothing can ever separate us from God's love. Neither death nor life, neither angels, demons, neither our fears for today nor our worries about tomorrow – not even the powers of hell can separate us from God's love. No power in the sky above or in the earth below – indeed, nothing in all creation will ever be able to separate us from the love of God that is revealed in Christ Jesus our Lord.** ROMANS 8:38-39-NLT

Chapter Sixteen

A Sliver of Light

As I've mentioned, my brother from New Zealand had been staying with us over the Christmas period. A few days prior to the fire he and Rick were looking at an old coin. They were having fun, laughing, and joking together. In hindsight this would become the type of normalcy I longed for.

A few days after the fire my brother casually stated he was going to look for the coin. I imagined him rummaging through the sea of ash becoming increasingly distressed. I believed he was clutching at straws and would be sorely disappointed. My eldest daughter offered to accompany him. I think she saw the distressed look on my face and knew I was worried for him.

A few hours later they returned grinning from ear to ear. Their laughter and the lightness on their faces, at such a dark time, is something I will never forget. Not only had they miraculously found the coin, but my daughter also found a wad of cash. The cash had been hidden in a drawer in a bedside table. Although the bedside table was a pile of ash the money had been protected by a sheet of good old-fashioned wallpaper. Even though this was a miniscule discovery, compared to what we had lost, it somehow restored my hope. Even though my walkie talkie was covered in ash and dirt, and the reception was distorted and crackly, God was reminding me that even amidst the most tumultuous grief, there is light and hope. Their laughter and lightness chipped away at my dark armour of grief. A sliver of light broke through.

> **The light shines in the darkness, and the darkness has not overcome it. JOHN 1:5 – NIV**

Chapter Seventeen

AN UNUSUAL CHRISTMAS CARD

P rior to the tragic events on Christmas Day a dear Christian friend sent me a Christmas card with a Bible verse. The verse was not a typical Christmas greeting and seemed strangely out of place.

> **When you go through deep waters and great trouble, I will be with you. When you go through rivers of difficulty, you will not drown! When you walk through the fire of oppression, you will not be burned up - the flames will not consume you.** Isaiah 43:2 - TLB

Unbeknownst to my friend, I had been given the same scripture in my walkie talkie times. God was trying to tell me something. He knew what was just around the corner and wanted to prepare me ahead of time. I knew God often used other people to convey or confirm walkie talkie messages.

A week after the house fire I remembered the card. It was no longer an odd Christmas card with an out-of-place verse. I knew God was speaking directly to me. I literally witnessed ferocious flames engulf our home. I felt I was drowning in a river of grief. I had no capacity to deal with losing my husband and the girls' father so tragically, or losing our family home and all our possessions.

Thankfully, I had not discarded my walkie talkie. I gingerly pressed the *Help* button begging God to somehow comfort me amidst this overwhelming grief.

An image popped into my mind. It was a picture of a ball. I had imagined rolling my body tightly into a ball until I was in the foetal position, so I related strongly to this image. I suggested to God He could then roll me, like a ball, out of my living nightmare to a land of sunshine, lollipops, and rainbows. Although I pummelled the *Help* button asking for this miracle to occur, it didn't.

I continued to offer helpful suggestions. "Okay, God. I get you aren't going to roll me to a better place, so how about you roll the grief away from me? That's a clever idea, isn't it?" *Silence.*

I was to learn grief was the price I paid for love. I could not be rolled away from grief, nor could grief be rolled away from me. I could not go over, around, or under it. I had to go *through* my grief.

I was reminded of a Bible verse I learned in Sunday School. It was tailor-made for my situation.

> **Even though I walk through the valley of the shadow of death I will fear no evil, for you are with me; your rod and your staff, they comfort me. You prepare a table before me in the presence of my enemies.** PSALM 23:4 - NIV

As well as having to go *through* my grief another word from the verse jumped out at me. The word *walk* was important. I knew God was saying I had to *walk through* the shadow of Rick's death. Again I howled in sheer desperation. "You've got to be kidding me, God. Isn't it enough to have to go through this tormenting grief? Now you expect me to walk as well? You know I don't have the energy to crawl, let alone walk."

Despite my creative plans, with the rolling and the ball, God stuck with His plan. He wanted me to *walk through* that dark valley. There was an exceptionally bright pledge attached. He promised He would be with me all the way. I made a deal with God. I told Him I would try to walk if He helped me to stand.

The unusual verse on my Christmas card, and the Psalm I learned in Sunday school, were God's walkie talkie messages to me during that overwhelming time. They became the life buoys I clung to for survival.

Chapter Eichteen

FEATHERED FRIENDS

When Rick and I moved from the mainland of Townsville to Magnetic Island I was horrified to learn we had inherited a family of wild kookaburras. They had the audacity to live in the gum trees surrounding our property. Frankly, I would have preferred a yard full of rusted-out cars. I'd had an intense bird phobia since childhood.

While showing us through the house the previous owner enthusiastically shared stories about the resident kookaburras coming to the patio for their daily feed. He took us to the patio where two wild kookaburras were sitting on *our* handrail waiting to be fed. Rick was chuffed with the idea of sharing his new home with some feathered friends. I was not at all chuffed. Rick offered to feed the kookaburras while I watched from a very safe distance.

I would love to tell you that once we moved into our lovely home my fear of birds abated, but that was not the case. I watched Rick feed the kookaburras morning after morning. I was content to prepare their meals but continued to observe cautiously from inside the house.

This routine continued for months until Rick decided he was going to leave a meat tray in the backyard for the kookaburras rather than hand-feed them. That was the plan, but it soon became apparent the kookaburras did not approve of a buffet. They preferred à la carte. Within a matter of days they stopped coming for breakfast.

Surprisingly, I missed their daily patio visits. I also missed their sunny disposition and raucous, heart-warming laughter. The house did not seem the same without them. I found myself worrying, hoping nothing had happened to them. I chuckled to myself; I was literally suffering from empty-nest syndrome.

I regretted I had allowed fear to prevent me from hand-feeding them. I shared this regret with Rick and promised to feed them if they returned. The days turned to weeks with still no sight or sound of our feathered family. Rick decided to stand on our back veranda and warble his kookaburra call which certainly amused our neighbours. Morning after morning he trilled like a bird, hoping the kookaburras would return. Eventually, we came to terms with the fact they had found another à la carte restaurant.

Months passed, and one morning a lone kookaburra flew onto the handrail as if she had never left. Within minutes, a second kookaburra was beside her. I felt a rush of adrenaline from sheer excitement rather than fear. It was then I realised I would have to keep my promise about feeding them, and the fear quickly returned.

Rick knew I was scared and he also knew I wanted to overcome this fear. Each time I fed the kookaburras Rick stood close behind me, protecting and supporting me. I wonder if part of his all-encompassing tactic was to ensure I did not bolt. Rick held my shaking hands in his as I moved them tentatively towards the huge, sharp, hungry beaks squawking for food. As time went by, I was comfortable enough to feed them on my own. I had formed a bond with these delightful creatures. Our bond became so strong I taught them to sit on my arm and shoulder.

Over the next several years our feathered family grew from two to seven. I came up with a novel idea to identify who was who; I painted their talons with assorted colours of nail polish. I am sure they were the envy of all the other kookaburras on the island who wished they could also attend *Salon de Sedon.*

It may sound strange, but the kookaburras became part of our family. They visited us twice a day for five years. Mauve, my favourite kookaburra, could be recognised by his purple nail polish. He often 'helped' me do the gardening. While I was digging and weeding and clipping he sat on my shoulder. His eagle eye (or kookaburra eye) swiftly spotted any worms in the soil and gulped them down.

Our precious feathered family were affected by the house fire on Christmas night. My heart ached for them as I noticed Mauve and the rest of the flock circling above what was once their landing pad, confused as to why they could no longer land and enjoy their restaurant meal. They flapped their wings wildly, overcome by heat and smoke. Their shrill screeches broke my heart. I felt like a mother watching her children suffer. Their simple, predictable world had changed overnight.

Every morning for the next six weeks I went to the site, which was once our family home, and fed my feathered friends. They came every day excitedly waiting to be fed. They sat in the trees over the property waiting for me to arrive and then flew down to greet me. Our relationship had not changed. They still trusted me, sitting on my arm and shoulder and eating from my hand. I gained indescribable comfort from our special bond. Having some semblance of normality and a daily routine also helped immensely. At least something in my upside-down world was normal and predictable.

Many caring people on Magnetic Island were concerned I was torturing myself by visiting the remains of the house. I knew they were right, but I did not want to disappoint my feathered family. As time went by it became increasingly difficult to enter the pile of rubble which had once been our home. Frequently seeing the location where Rick had died was harrowing. I realised visiting the site was probably contributing to my frequent flashbacks.

I decided to do what I always do when I am stuck. I would talk to God about it. I dug out my walkie talkie which was dusty and covered in ash. I spoke from my heart, pouring out my pain and confusion for my kookaburra family's plight. I also shared how hard it was for me to let go of the precious memories Rick and I had made with our feathered family. Within a matter of days my walkie talkie chat paid off. I had a peace about giving myself one last week with the kookaburras.

The final visit came, and I said goodbye to my dear friends with tears in my eyes. I wished I could explain to them what I had to do and why. As I started to leave, the kookaburras did something I will never forget. They encircled me, north, south, east, and west; some in tree branches, others on power poles, some on the neighbour's roof. They joined together and sang like I'd never heard them sing. They were like a choir of angels crooning a heavenly chorus from the depths of their souls. I sensed their song was one of thanks and one of endings, a goodbye song.

Again, some would call this a coincidence, but I believe it was a God-incidence. I believe God orchestrated this fond farewell. After all, the Holy Spirit is represented as a bird, a dove, so God obviously has a soft spot for birds as well. He also cares about the tiniest sparrow so why wouldn't he care for the kookaburras?

As I left my home, one last time, I knew my kookaburra family would be just fine. I was grateful for their heart-felt goodbye song and the fact I could leave them on a happy note.

> **Look at the birds of the air; they do not sow or reap or store away in barns, and yet your heavenly Father feeds them.**
> MATTHEW 6:26 - NIV

God knew how much I loved the kookaburras and cared about their welfare. I knew I could talk to Him about anything, big or small.

Interestingly, I feel God's love in a unique way when He answers my small prayers. It's like a reminder He really is with me in every aspect of my life.

JONAH 4:11 clearly shows God was concerned about the animals as well as the people.

Have there been times in your life when you haven't talked to God about something because you thought it was too small or insignificant? God is interested in every aspect of your life.

CHAPTER NINETEEN

MESSAGE IN MOVIELAND

I lived in an altered reality for months after losing Rick, and our family home. Thankfully, we were surrounded by caring family and friends who provided as much support and comfort as they could.

Overall, this period of time was a blur. The nights were no longer a time for sleep and repose, but a time of bitter pain and loneliness. My tears seemed to flow from an endless supply. At times, the tears brought a sense of relief to my tense body but my mind could not rest. I had constant flashbacks; flames engulfing our home, discovering Rick's lifeless body. The reels played continuously on a massive screen in my mind.

During this time I began to watch real movies, many, many movies. I needed something to replace the flashbacks. A movie could transport me to another place and time, a place I called *Movieland*. *Movieland* provided respite from the pervasive grief that had overtaken my life.

One day in *Movieland* I had a life-changing moment. One of the characters in a movie was being interviewed by a reporter about a horrific experience. The reporter asked her how it felt being a victim. She simply responded, "I am not a victim. I am a survivor." Those words resonated with me loudly and clearly. I heard the walkie talkie click, **"Jen, you need to have a survivor's mentality."**

These are not words I would personally use. I knew God was speaking to me. The unusual message immediately found a home in my heart. I realised God was sending a message of wisdom and direction amidst my pain. The words gave me hope and strength. I felt as though God was beside me, speaking the words directly to me.

It would have been easy and understandable to remain a victim after what happened to my husband, my girls, my possessions, and myself. Believe me, I threw many pity-parties-for-one. The catering wasn't great, neither was the company. To hear those words, **"Jen, you need to have a survivor's mentality"** was exactly what I needed to pull me out of the miry pit. I realised there was no other way to get through this. It was a choice: pity-parties-for-one or think, speak, and act like a survivor.

Chapter Twenty

MY KNIGHT IN TARNISHED ARMOUR

After Rick's death I experienced debilitating *mourning-sickness* for about six months. This type of *mourning-sickness* was far worse than any morning-sickness I had experienced during my pregnancies. After his death, my workplace became a haven as I was dealing with guests and visitors who knew nothing of what had taken place. I could retreat from curious stares, whispers, and people bombarding me with insensitive questions. This often happens to family members after someone has taken their life. My reception desk became my fortress, putting a barrier between me and the rest of the world. I was once again *Jen* and not *Jen who had that awful thing happen to her*. I loved the fact that I could happily greet the guests and make their stay as pleasant as possible. I saw this as my therapy. I was also thinking, acting, and behaving like a Survivor.

After a hellish six months of *mourning-sickness* I finally felt ready to board the train and leave Mourning-Ville. My wounded heart was in recovery mode, my sleep deprived body was starting to rest, I was regaining weight, and my thoughts weren't fixated on the night of the fire. It was a wonderful feeling to board the train and watch Mourning-Ville become a speck in the distance.

Just as my *mourning-sickness* was lifting I received the devastating news that one of my dearest friends, Irene, had passed away in New Zealand. We had been friends for over 20 years. While she was in remission from cancer, she had come to visit me in Australia. She knew the disease would shorten her life, but she believed she would live until the age of 60. I had desperately wanted to believe her because it meant I would have time to visit her in New Zealand before she passed away.

Irene was 46 when she died. Her untimely death shocked me to the core. I had lost my opportunity to say goodbye and thank her for being such a wonderful friend. I wanted to attend her funeral, but I was not mentally or emotionally strong enough so soon after Rick's death.

After she passed away I spoke to her husband, Rob, on the phone. Rob and I had also been friends for decades. I knew too well what he was going through, and I also knew there was nothing I could do to ease his pain. As I ended the call a tidal wave of emotion hit me. This was simply not fair. It was too much, especially so soon after Rick's death.

For the first time since Rick's passing I was angry with God. I was also angry with Rick. He had known Irene. I wanted him to be with me to comfort me. I wanted us to be able to share the memories we had of Irene. I desperately craved his love and support.

I would soon discover Irene's death was my tipping point. I spiralled into dark and lonely places. I became like a stranger in a bizarre, twisted landscape. The nights were unbearable. To avoid being alone in my room I walked the deserted streets of Magnetic Island for hours on end.

I had always loved how Rick hugged me and I longed to feel his arms around me. In an attempt to escape the harsh reality of my life my mind reverted to a child-like state, a fairy-tale state. I began to dream of knights and castles and fair maidens being rescued. In this instance I was the fair maiden who needed rescuing. I pictured my knight galloping along and whisking me up gallantly and effortlessly. Naturally, we would ride off into the sunset and have our own happily ever after. BAM...down to earth I plummeted. I did not know any knights.

Because I was also without a home my sense of disenfranchisement was exacerbated. Although I had been living with my daughter I did not want to take her generosity for granted. She also had backpackers staying with her which often meant her house was crowded. As much as I appreciated her kindness, and having a place to stay, I longed to have my own space where I could simply be *Jen*.

My knight in shining armour visions resurfaced. I recalled a friend I had helped through a challenging time. I contacted him and shared what had happened. He immediately comforted me and seemed to understand. He realised I needed my own space and offered me a place to stay in his home.

My knight's castle became a home away from home. I could be myself and have a sense of normalcy. He let me feel what I needed to feel and gave me total freedom. Knowing I had somewhere I could simply be *Jen*, without troubling my family, was wonderfully soothing. My knight had a great sense of humour which I found refreshing. It was also a distraction from the very heavy emotions I was carrying.

As time passed, I began to have a niggling sense that my relationship with my knight in tarnished armour was not in my best interests. During a walkie talkie time God confirmed this when he whispered, ***"Clean cut."*** I knew the meaning was clear, I was to end the relationship with my knight. However, ending the friendship with my knight was a process which took longer than anticipated. It was like walking a tightrope, 10 steps forward and five steps back.

Obviously, God saw my struggle and how difficult I was finding it to make a clean cut. He gave me another message, in picture form, which greatly encouraged me. The vision was a pair of scissors cutting through a piece of paper one tiny snip at a time. It dawned on me that my relationship with my knight would end slowly, little by little, snip by snip instead of one major cut. God was being gracious to me and meeting me where I was. My friendship with my knight did end, and it ended slowly, one snip at a time.

My knight was not legendary, nor was he the stuff of fairy tales. He was human. Although his armour was tarnished and dented, he still had noble qualities for which I will always be grateful. He comforted me through an extremely difficult and lonely time and he made me laugh. I fondly thought of him as my Sir Laughs-a-Lot rather than my Sir Lancelot.

Was I in love with him? Definitely not. Nor did he love me. We had a mutual friendship and supported one another. God knew my heart was broken and that I longed for male companionship. However, he also knew what was best for me. Thankfully, during our walkie talkie times He gently guided me out of a relationship that could have caused me added grief in the long run.

I realised even though God understood my pain, and the reasons I sought solace with my earthly knight, His standards do not change. These standards come from a place of love and wisdom. God showed me I was looking for a quick-fix. I was also looking at my situation from an earthly perspective, rather than an eternal one.

I also learned He was my One True Knight in Shining Armour. The depth of love and comfort I needed could not be provided in human form.

Chapter Twenty-One

THE ANCHOR HOLDS

During my time of heartbreaking grief, and my tours-for-one from dusk till dawn, I received a walkie talkie message. It consisted of just three words **"The Anchor Holds."** Those three words were a lifeline. I felt like a tiny boat on a vast ocean being tossed back and forth in a never-ending storm. The thought of God being my anchor, keeping me steady and strong when I felt so disoriented and alone, was exactly what I needed.

I remembered a song I loved; *The Anchor Holds*. I desperately needed to hear it. Any reprieve from my grief was welcome. I knew the song was on a CD I had given to someone many years prior when her husband was terminally ill. I did not feel comfortable asking her to return it.

Several months later I went to New Zealand for a holiday. This was the first time in 28 years I had been home without Rick by my side. Although I enjoyed being with family and friends I was terribly lonely. I was with people who loved and cared for me, but I was also experiencing fresh waves of grief, having come to terms with the fact Rick was not there. I also felt extremely guilty that I was alive and he was not.

As my holiday continued, wonderful memories flooded back. They brought momentary joy, to be followed by overwhelming sadness. While sightseeing I often turned around, waiting for Rick to catch up. I started to point out something he would have been interested in, only to realise he wasn't there. The waves of grief smashed mercilessly, knocking me down and dragging me under.

One particularly rough day, I was visiting friends. One of them wanted me to watch a Christian teaching with him. As I moved to a comfy chair I felt the walkie talkie click, **"The Anchor Holds."** I laughed, "God, are you telling me this video is going to be about an anchor?" Moments later the title flashed on the screen, *God, our Anchor in Times of Trouble.*

Later that evening I told my dear friend, Lyn, how lost and alone I felt. I also mentioned the song, *The Anchor Holds* and how God had used it to remind me He was my anchor. A smile crossed Lyn's face, "We have that CD somewhere, not sure where, but we do have it." Despite it being midnight Lyn, John (her husband) and I searched everywhere for the CD but couldn't find it. We had given up hope when my walkie talkie clicked, **"Get up and look again."** You guessed it, Jen's catchphrase was the response, "God, you've got to be kidding me!" I looked at the vast collection before me yet again when I noticed a CD with no cover. I opened it to discover it was the one we had been searching for.

Whenever I hear *The Anchor Holds* tears stream down my face. It describes the pain I felt and how tattered and torn I was emotionally, spiritually, mentally, and physically. It also reminds me of God's promise to anchor me and keep me steady when I feel I'm going under.

Anyone younger than 25 is probably wondering why I didn't just Google the song, or have it on my playlist. In the 'olden days' no such luxury existed. I needed the CD to play on my CD player.

Finding the CD may seem like another coincidence. I know it was a God-incidence, particularly having received the message, **"Look again"** from God.

My experience shows how powerful the right song can be. God can use music to reach to the depths of our souls, healing our wounds in a miraculous manner.

The Anchor Holds
(Chorus)

The anchor holds though the ship is battered
The anchor holds though the sails are torn
I have fallen on my knees as I faced the raging seas
The anchor holds
In spite of the storm

Songwriters: Ray Boltz, Lawrence Mendel Jr. Chewning

Chapter Twenty-Two

FLAT BATTERY

Although God had reminded me to have a survivor's mentality, rather than a victim's mentality, this was easier said than done. I struggled mentally and emotionally and often felt I was drifting without a purpose. To put it plainly, my battery was flat.

Have you ever jumped in your car, turned the key, and encountered resistance? I felt like that. I wanted to move, I wanted to tune in to God, but no matter how hard I tried that battery wasn't working. I tried reading the Bible but the words were a blur and nothing made sense. I tried praying but often ended up in tears or falling asleep.

This challenging time taught me that God can still speak to me when my walkie talkie battery is flat. Ironically, the message I received when I had a flat battery was, **"Rest and recharge."** He was telling me I needed to put my walkie talkie on its base to recharge. I needed to come back to base and back to basics.

The scripture He gave me was:

> **Be still and know that I am God.**
> PSALM 46:10 - NIV

Apart from my **"Rest and recharge"** message, and the wonderful Psalm, initially I didn't receive many messages from God during my recharge period. There was a very simple reason for this; we both knew I wasn't expecting Him to speak to me. I was so depleted I didn't have the faith or the energy to listen. However, I did have enough faith to know He could listen to me.

The *Expectancy* button on my walkie talkie was pressed repeatedly. I wasn't expecting much but God honoured the tiny amount of faith I had. I was reminded of the mustard seed faith Jesus talked about.

I realised many of my recharging requirements came down to physical rest and sleep. We can be so spiritually minded we forget about our basic human needs like healthy eating, drinking enough water, resting and decent quality sleep. I desperately needed rest and sleep. Instead of fighting this I gave myself permission to lie down and rest.

During my rest times I often listened to podcasts. I found great inspiration from three teachers in particular: Bayless Conley, Joyce Meyer, and Rick Warren. Simple words and phrases leapt out, planting themselves in the arid areas of my heart. Over time, I noticed the bars on my charger flicker and turn green. My heart, mind and spirit were being recharged simply by resting and listening to positive messages; messages that were in line with God's Life Manual, the Bible.

Another battery booster was listening to and singing praise songs. The Bible tells us to put on the garment of praise for the spirit of heaviness. I certainly had a heavy spirit and some heavy attitudes. I gladly exchanged my garments of grief, sadness, anger, and frustration for God's exquisite garment of praise. I had to make a choice to *put on* the garment of praise.

I felt recharged not only from listening to songs but by singing to God. Even the lyrics from a non-Christian song can be custom-made into a personalised prayer. Because Christian music isn't always accessible in everyday life, I have learnt to take the words of applicable songs and turn them into a prayer.

One song in particular resonated with me. Rod Stewart's *Have I told you lately that I love you?* seemed to open my heart to God again. God knew I loved Him, and He also knew I was so worn down that words failed me. The words of this song seemed tailor-made for me and I often sang the chorus to God.

Have I told you lately that I love you. Did you know there's no one else above you. You fill my heart with gladness, take away all my sadness, ease my troubles that's what you do.

Talking out loud was another battery booster. Instead of just contemplating prayers, scriptures and promises God had given me, I spoke them out loud. This gave me a new zest for life and sparked something within me. I often coupled talking and walking. I always wore headphones so if passers-by heard me they would think I was on the phone.

A simple, yet important battery booster is good old authenticity and honesty. We often pretend we're okay when we're not. It's easy to prattle on with our super-spiritual lingo around people, but we can't fool God. God has heard me rant and rave countless times. He has also had to put up with my endless questions and of course my catchphrase, "God, you've got to be kidding me!"

God knows what's hidden in my heart so there's no point putting on a spiritual front. In fact, I often feel a reassuring sense of peace when I'm real with God. It's as if He's saying, **"There you go, Jen. Doesn't it feel good to get that off your chest?"** The Holy Spirit is the great

Counsellor after all. Honesty removes battery corrosion and re-establishes a clear connection.

Being in a pleasant place or environment boosts my battery. I love the beach, the ocean, looking at the night sky, and going for nature walks. I feel close to God in these places and seem to recharge very quickly.

Feel free to use, and add to, my recharging tips!

Expectancy - even if your faith is small

Rest

Sleep

Listening to podcasts

Listening to praise and worship songs

singing personalised love songs to God

Singing praise and worship songs

Speaking scriptures and promises out loud

Honesty

A pleasant environment

Chapter Twenty-Three

MOURN NO MORE

I would love to say everything I hear during my walkie talkie times makes perfect sense. Alas, that is not always the case.

During one of my walkie talkie times I received an unusual message. The message was, **"Mourn no more."** Naturally, I reverted to my familiar catchphrase, "You've got to be kidding me, God. That's not how this grieving thing works. There's no *Off* switch. And anyway, I'm not even sure this is You. Maybe it's my mind playing tricks on me. I'm going to have to do a Gideon again and ask you to give me confirmation, please."

As I began my quiet time with God, I opened the daily reading from Samuel 16:1. The heading for the reading was, "It's time to move on." Not only was the heading relatable, but the content of the daily reading was about grief. Samuel was mourning the loss of King Saul when God told him it was time to move on. This was certainly confirmation for me, another God-incidence, not simply a coincidence.

I wish I could say I was grateful for this message but I was not at all grateful. I was stunned. As tears rolled down my cheeks I reminded God

I had done so much crying there was no point stopping. I even pictured a lake in heaven, *Lake Jen-Jen,* overflowing with my tears.

While skimming through my Bible one day I came across PSALM 56:8 which I had not previously seen. **"You keep track of all my sorrows. You have collected all my tears in your bottle. You have recorded each one in your book."** I felt like God was speaking directly to me.

An incredible sense of peace washed over me. In addition to owning a lake in Heaven, I imagined having a shelf stacked with hundreds of bottles of my tears. Although God's message and meaning were direct, suggesting I *Mourn no More,* this Psalm reminded me God was not being harsh. He understood the depth of my pain and my tears were precious to Him. He was trying to help me in the midst of my pain.

Having God confirm His message gave me much-needed strength. I was able to make a conscious decision to reset my heart's compass. No longer would it point towards *Grieve Forever.* Instead, it would point towards *Jen's True North.* It was time to stop looking in the rear-view mirror and drive forward.

Not long after, I had an idea that did not seem extremely helpful. I had an urge to pack away any photos of Rick. The photos sometimes evoked happy memories. More often than not, they caused tormenting thoughts and emotions. The photos triggered memories of Rick's after-shave scent and the touch of his hand. I often stared at the photos, begging Rick for answers that would never come. "Why? Why? Why? Why did you do it?"

The next step in my mourn-no-more journey came via a dream. It was so vivid that it woke me during the night. In my dream, a fierce whirlwind came into my bedroom and blew open the doors of my wardrobe. There were clothes in the wardrobe, but there were also two cremation urns stored within: Rick's urn and another urn belonging to a dear friend, Ray.

Every aspect of the dream was true. Naturally, I had clothes in my wardrobe. Strangely enough, I also had two cremation urns stored there. It had become a standard joke in our household that if you were male, and your name began with 'R' you should stay away from Jen or you might end up in an urn in her wardrobe.

The morning after my dream, my daughter was waiting for me in the kitchen. "Mum, I think you and I need to have a talk." This was indeed a role reversal. She continued, "I feel it's time that you scattered dad's ashes." It was then that I recalled my whirlwind dream. I knew this was a God-incidence, not a coincidence, and I was being given the next step to help me to move through the grief.

Over the next couple of weeks I scattered Rick's and Ray's ashes at their favourite bays on Magnetic Island. I kept some of Rick's ashes and drove from one end of the island to the other wondering what to do with them. A walkie talkie time gave me much-needed clarity; I was to place them in the Remembrance Wall at our local cemetery.

Naturally, like most people who grieve, I found some days harder than others. A picture God gave me at the time fortifies me to this day. I received an image of a dead-end street. The street was filled with deep potholes and derelict houses. The message was loud and clear, **"Jen, don't go down that street "** I knew God was telling me not to go down the street of despair by reliving the events of Rick's death.

That simple picture and phrase have kept me from despair so many times. To this day, when tempted to re-live the trauma, I say to myself, "Jen, don't go down that street " I'm so grateful my walkie talkie faith means

I have a Guide who directs me firmly, compassionately, and lovingly. He knows what I need so much more than I do.

> **Do not remember former things, nor consider things of the past. Here I am, doing a new thing; now it is springing up - do you not know about it? I will surely make a way in the desert, rivers in the wasteland.** ISAIAH 43:18-29 - TLB

When God gives me a picture or a phrase it has such a lasting impact. The old adage "A picture speaks a thousand words" has certainly been true for me. Countless times I have recalled the lifesaving words: **"Jen, don't go down that street."** Picturing the dead-end street immediately helps me refocus and prevents me going down the rabbit hole.

Chapter Twenty-Four

OVER AND OUT

Thank you for reading some of my walkie talkie adventures. I hope my experiences reassure you that God can meet you exactly where you're at. He wants to speak to you whether you're on top of the world, or you don't know which way is up. God wants a heart-to-heart connection with you regardless of your circumstances.

Whether this type of relationship with God is new to you, or you're an experienced walkie talkie operator, you may want to keep track of your walkie talkie conversations with God. If so, let me encourage you (not pester you) to start your own Walkie Talkie Adventure Journal.

> My heart has heard you say, "Come and talk with me." And my heart responds, "Lord, I am coming."
> Psalm 27:8 - TLB

God will not make you listen to Him, speak to Him, or believe in Him. He has given you the gift of free will.

He wants to get to know you, but He will never be forceful or pushy. He will knock to try and get your attention, but if you don't want to answer the door He won't push it down, or force His way in.

> **Here I am! I stand at the door and knock. If anyone hears my voice and opens the door, I will come in and eat with that person, and they with me. REVELATION 3:20 - NIV**

Website: walkietalkiefaith.com

Email: walkietalkiefaith@gmail.com

www.ingramcontent.com/pod-product-compliance
Lightning Source LLC
Chambersburg PA
CBHW042319090526
44583CB00025BA/3172